WILLINGLY

Willingly

Poems
by
MARC FRAZIER

Adelaide Books
New York/Lisbon
2018

WILLINGLY
Poems
By Marc Frazier

Copyright © by Marc Frazier
Cover design © 2018 Adelaide Books

Published by Adelaide Books, New York / Lisbon
adelaidebooks.org

Editor-in-Chief
Stevan V. Nikolic

All rights reserved. No part of this book may be reproduced in any manner whatsoever without written permission from the author except in the case of brief quotations embodied in critical articles and reviews.

For any information, please address Adelaide Books
at info@adelaidebooks.org
or write to:
Adelaide Books
244 Fifth Ave. Suite D27
New York, NY, 10001

ISBN-10: 1-949180-52-2
ISBN-13: 978-1-949180-52-7

Printed in the United States of America

For Meg

Content

little death, dissociative identity *13*

If It Comes to That *14*

expose *15*

synopsis *16*

The Next Step *18*

awakening *19*

invitation *22*

Abide with Me *23*

architecture *24*

Heart Tide *25*

Transformación *26*

I am aware *27*

A Brief Journey: Double Etheree *29*

Meditation One *30*

November Evenings, Southern Illinois *32*

Then *33*

Do Not Weep *34*

Dakota, Illinois *36*

Geography Lessons *37*

Without Words *39*
Sergio *41*
Appositives *44*
The Whole Picture *46*
Want *47*
What's Missing *49*
Thanksgiving with the Homeless Men of Starbucks *50*
The Universe Expands *52*
These Three Remain *53*
Dog Days *55*
Danger *56*
Little Mexico *59*
August *60*
Without You *61*
Plea *62*
Math *63*
What is Left *65*
The Loss *66*
Into Dark: Cinquains *67*
Neighbor *68*
Links *69*
What is Unseen *71*
Iterations *73*
Christmas Eve *74*

Again *75*
The Waves *76*
Stories, Café Voltaire *78*
Willingly *80*
Taken *82*
The Trip to Uncle Harry's Funeral *84*
Theorem *86*
Listen *88*
Prayer in Winter *90*
infinitives *91*
Song of Songs *93*
Remainders *94*
Painting of Woman, Café Express *95*
Settling *96*
Over a Dark Lake *97*
Crossings *99*
Once upon a Time *101*
The Rock *103*
Progression *104*
Acknowledgments *107*
List of Credits *109*
About the Author *111*

We don't see things as they are.

We see them as we are.

—Anais Nin

little death, dissociative identity

at this moment of letting go
all of me works
together
in this place I most desire
who are you
who did you say
you were
does it matter who I am
you could be anyone
yet I remember your exactness
for a time
if I see you
again
I may not know you
I may not be
who you expect

If It Comes to That

> Every day you have less reason/not to give yourself away
> —Wendell Berry

Each thing like something else:
    the body: vessel as metaphor,
        its manifest of parts.

Eyes: blue reach of water.
    Your body chopping wood—a boastful ship.
        Alert, you are a seagull tracking fish.

The arc of a dolphin when you stretch.
    Swell of breath—what carries us through.
        The pull of horizon.

Your scent: loam in a plowed field.
    Sorrow heavy as the stones of cairns.
        Crooked path to the old forest.

What did you mean: this shattered hope?
    Do we fit in this landscape?
        In the deafening dusk do I fit in us?

expose

a sudden implosion and then nothing
but tunnels covered in bone dust

a hawk with a human grin looks down
as I pick up coins I'd buried in childhood

they smell of oak/smoke/pumpkin seed/
my mother's hands showed how much she worried

the form of her fears a tiny beast: black and shiny/
tops of wheat wave as the wind shifts clouds

and the moon comes out prematurely/
the dying sun is a month's worth of blood

smoothed on canvas/hillside in shadow/black stamens
alert, petals a yellow warmth/birdcall blooms—

waves of sound—a refrain evoking prayer/earth an edifice—
its backbone a witness—a barnful of solitude/your unholy

absence an artifact/we could not save us/gather the sea
faithful angels, the yellow stars/it is time I become who I am

synopsis

mother threatens to kill me
    during the seventh month of my life
great uncle John and my dad
    haul her screaming and clawing
into the car for the trip to Mercyville
    father left with three children to soothe
mother is admitted for insulin and
    electro-shock therapies
after her return
    father discovers how deep
her resentment can go how impossible
    to resume except for their duty
to have more children
    I am an altar boy
studying Latin
    family and the Church
everything
    I have to survive my father
a difficult battle to win
    I live as a person
divided
    the religious youth
and the man
    cruising men
my fragile self fueled

WILLINGLY

    by porn alcohol
and a woman
    I'd always been in love with
from the farmland
    to the coastal waters
where I finally
    fit into myself

The Next Step

How far you've gone
As my breath wraps in a blanket
memory shreds like a hunted grouse
shards of words powerless to touch us

Going anywhere reveals how I feel about where I've left
When man in the moon became literal
our language foundered for new metaphors
to describe that which is not only seen from afar

Surprising things happen to the narrow
path of my person
The dawn kindles/the cloak of sea dims
Where there is water there is more water:

the May queen's crown of flowers
on its delicate blue pillow
the starter pearls for my littlest sister
you sunk in the warm sand of my side

Wet peonies nod out of respect
Sparrows in the bath create tidal sweeps
in the final heat of October
I could build a life but the moon keeps changing
O sliver of a moon, O death.

awakening

parable of the
honeycomb:
                       accretion of labor,
                       queen at the height
of her powers,
pulse of the
                       hive audible, warm
                       aura of affirmation.
waterfowl, birdcall.
houses sleep
                       as ravens gather
                       morning
to weave
wings
                       with sky.
                       mute,
believers scatter
ashes—
                       witness to
                       plundered flesh.
bones in the earth
echo,
                       sun bathes
                       the surface
of water

in light.
                    lagoon, a cradle:
                    water lilies poise
for painting—
the illusion of stasis
                    where life sings:
                    the resurrection
and the light.
hillside in
                    shadow. roots
                    gather energy,
a poplar's nimbus
glows.
                    buds sparse
                    but insistent
in early spring.
herons clamor
                    over the lake.
                    a pilgrim's
new continent:
ocean of waving
                    grasses,
                    the weight
of vast spaces,
silence.

WILLINGLY

                remember
                the western
fires, sky ablaze
with the desire
                of destruction,
                (retribution:
ashes to ashes)
how we saved
                what we could,
                nothing more.

invitation

Winter here with me.
Your scent lingers
in the narrow valley of thighs,
something religious or mythic
breathing close by like a red wound.

I want hordes of flowers to watch over us.
We will share our breath with the rose, the iris,
drawn out of our drowse
like bees from their comb.

The room warms,
flowers stretch—
come for us.

Abide with Me

> …there is time for
> everything, everything is there not
> though the balance is
> difficult, is coming un-
> done
> —Jorie Graham

the earth/this body
alive
    how?
skin/organs
    each breath full
    for now
the desire to be
    seen/unseen
waves of suffering/waves of compassion
this moment
    kissing your thin mustache
I watch/we are watched
    floors collapse
I reach   for sanity
wake   to the scaffold of your body: an atrium of sorrow
    to someone else's day

architecture

eyes of wet blue shale
troughs of closed eyelids
the body's fever of warm adobe
gone the dead load of the past—its leftover swarf
what is hollow will often hold
your inner knee: the smooth comfort of a dovetail
the inner curve of thighs open
after—your face the high shine of terrazzo
I hear each cell crave to be more
my desire to be less
anchored deep in the kiln of your chest

Heart Tide

—from phrases of Denis Johnson's poems

I used to never be able to hear stars,
        the orchestra of clouds,
        the tide of the heart.

Loving you glows like yellow fires in yellow globes—
        brightness you might see
        bloom, coming over a hill into sun.

My clear heart rests in your hand,
        beyond death's fingers.
        It holds itself, freed of geography and time.

Loving you glows like two matches that will not go out.

Transformación

We kiss in tunnels as light waits, the narrow rail
curves, and the locomotive snakes us behind.
Giant, vertical rocks disappear. Sooty smoke over
a prairie dog town, a gorge deep as God.

I absorb this language where love and place are one:
    arroyo, respaldo…
            montaña, hombre…

After a lifetime of prairie, grass—there is scrub, *cañon,
chamisa*. I live in blue spilling over the *Sangre de Cristos*,
Cochiti, into the Rio Grande Gorge, sleep the silver
nights of Santa Fe beside the landscape I most desire.

I am aware

of her claim: *wife*
the earth   solid as an oath

vertebrae, organs   each full breath
this moment
          brain coiled in skull

your black mustache

midnight   you turn into a husband
in dreams I am aware

of wings that beat, bloody and useless
        I reach

    as story after story collapses under me
    below—the blue pool of ocean

in my childhood home
    I search for the right room

        for my parents' faces   before they
were
my second skin lies beside me

Marc Frazier

I wake to waves of sound, light among which I blur
    to your absence

Am I a body warming to its new heart

    or a heart newly harvested

        for someone else's desire to be?

A Brief Journey: Double Etheree

still
water
lily pad
surface light rip-
ples, distant birdcall
a skull in ashes peers
hollow eyes haunt the thick air
old woods with prayers on its breath
deeper in, solitude, a cleared path
a home cradled in a nest of moonlight

metaphor for asylum, body stilled
hieroglyphs—bird scratchings in dry earth
the way back to mystery's edge
morning rises clear, godlike
a steeple of regrets
falls, frees memory
ever mortal
certain lips
whisper
yes

Meditation One

What we spoke of at those times—
ordinary things like the weather,

the inner life of Midwesterners rarely spoken of.
Self-reflection a luxury of the lazy.

We sat outside so much growing up—
on the front porch, in the yard,

often before, during, or after a storm.

I remember mostly times with mother
who was usually in motion—a cracked artifact patched—

visibly stronger and more beautiful.
My sibs and I competed for her favor.

In our house there was always a storm before calm.
There is a great silence where she once sat,

so loud it is deafening.

WILLINGLY

A family fractures and no one can tell by looking at its parts.
We are the cracked trees of our youths' ice storm

scattered throughout a broken world.
Where is the peace we were promised?

Why do I think that promise had been made—

November Evenings, Southern Illinois

Shadows cast a Hereford's markings across your profile.
You grind flour, burn the squash, and laugh.

Evening, you tilt your hat. It makes no difference.
You say you don't belong, throw dice, take back promises as
easily as that.

I listen to wind in the eaves.
End of season here—cold chases away the fickle, pink legs.

Neighbors chip paint from their house.
Lovers embrace on the roof, whisper.

The world below brims with remarks they choose to ignore.

Then

Weren't we young together?
Didn't we grope in beer-soaked rooms,
patios, parking lots…
Didn't we want it
more than anything?
Together alone at the Image:
screen full of cocks, asses—
theatre of sex and death—
men bent over the back row.
What mattered then:
the sudden surge in the dark,
the end of love in a land of half-life.
Weren't we ready for the next?
A body to die for.
Didn't we?

Do Not Weep

The willow is slow to bud
despite the warmth.
How tricky it is to bring a thing to life—
to deliver, emphatically,
a thing that lasts for a time:
what we are given.

Death happens.
You say prayers and lower a body
to be stuck forever
to be stripped of flesh—
think of that.

As a child the absent were always there.
Where were my mother's parents, my father's mother?
And there were those leaving in their padded caskets:
Tante Edo, Aunt Bertha, Uncle Bud—
a chain of the dead strung out like beads on a rosary.

Have faith in the willow:
its roots tenacious like some people who last.

WILLINGLY

There is no finality: no terminal bud ever grows
like us who continue in a different form.

The Japanese say that a ghost is at home
where a willow grows.
We are home in the here, now.
There is no birth, no death.
Just the bright badge of our moment.

Dakota, Illinois

Elvis died that day. A bad omen. I did not get the teaching job. In a small greasy spoon after the interview I stirred diminishing options into my coffee. I'd driven the length of Illinois, south to north, to this tiny farm town. When pop icons die, we mourn the loss of our own aspirations, say they die too young, fear our number's almost up. What I'm telling you could be the truth. I need proof I was once young. I need to be inspired. *Love is never enough, I tell you. Not even in the greatest of novels.* A friend of mine wrote that and I still hate her for it. I need more truths like this. I am not in a generous mood much of the time. Once I wrote, *It is hard to distinguish what we lack from greed.* I remember feeling clever but that is never enough. There is another truth: *I have lied in poems just to sound good.* Is that authentic enough for you? Can you trust me now? How close can we get, I wonder, you and I?

Geography Lessons

Tulips, hats like wings,
Wooden shoes, water in between
Everything.

A young country with resources,
I want to rise up
but take each of father's assaults.

And she is putting out fires
on all fronts.

Dogs with little barrels,
Snowy mountains, chocolate.

I am the spoils of father's campaign.
My voice silenced, his words
the only language.

He believes in this land:
It is flat and you can get anywhere
On foot. Eventually.

Humidity dripping. Insects. Houses
On stilts. Water filled with danger.

Marc Frazier

The woman at the little store smiles,
Says I have big, blue eyes.
I do not know this.

Two blocks away, she is another country.

Without Words

> The body contains the life story just as much as the brain.
> —Edna O'Brien

Even now I stiffen when you hug me,
frozen in an infant's body memory.

Each word I write aims to uncover the damage,
to express trauma that happens before language.

But a body remembers what happened.
How I want to surrender, to let you reach me:

My body's wanting to love is not the same as loving
though wanting to be loved is the same as loving.

For seven months your crazed depression
nursed me as if the cord had never been cut.

When you threatened my life they hauled you away
like one of your drunken uncles from childhood.

There is no such thing as closure,
nor did we find that new opening that rewrites trauma.

Marc Frazier

The body will have what it will and never let go.
Still, other selves survive.

There is not enough light to bring us into it together.
But almost.

Sergio

> I fall apart every time I think of you swallowed by the dark.
> —Joni Mitchell

I'm seeing a man who is wealthy and traveled
and everything
      you are not.

The linen is fine and for breakfast we have tea from Harrods.
When we dine, we charm the waiter
with our wit and urbanity
      and leave a big tip.

And from his place on the seventeenth floor
I have a tremendous view of the city in which
      I loved you.

I can't believe how many windows I've
looked through in my life.
I'm in a trance on the "L" as we rumble along, swaying.
      There is no end to seeing and riding trains

and walking icy streets and climbing stairs to tiny rooms
where men do anything because of biology
      and dark places in the mind.

Marc Frazier

And there is no end to these steps in the movie
where I kill you with my lust, prowl the dirty
      floors, the cold cement, the bitter middle

of a Chicago night, the more I have sex, the more
I get even. I forget life has little to do with us
and know that you go on.

When I saw you last, you hung your head while I stood
solicitous, touching you as if I always would.
      The scars still there, on your chin,

on the left edge of your lip—
a car crash you had said. Imperfections.
      None of this has happened if it has
      anything to do with me.

I distance myself from you, a movie camera pulling back.
If this were the movies, I'd run into
you as we hailed the same cab.
      But I've stopped going to movies.

After we make a tame kind of love, I
look over the wall of his side
at the glowing clock and wonder where,

WILLINGLY

among millions, you are.
      In the morning when he awakes,

I'm already studying the skyline,
scanning the city, my desire for sex with anyone rising
as I try once again to hold or break you, to let you go.

Appositives

A martyr in ecstatic bloom—air white waves
of ephemera—stranded on the island
of God, transient, heart immaculate,
complete.

Phlox laden with heavy scent,
nameless fields under moonlight,
stars, dawn over the pinewoods,
light from the yellow
iris, brush dry as old
bones, the plundered
flesh.

A gull's refrain echoes in my sleep,
lit windows beckon the children of fable,
red fox lurking, memories—
salt in a wound, silver
fish that slip away.

The willow's erotic sway ripples
the air, always the shore
beckons in my dreams,
a shallow breath is borne
to the singing
wind—the captive

WILLINGLY

secret—artifact of the past,
light on water, birdcall.

Can I abandon self for once?
Who will remember me?
Watchful mountains in the distance,
I utter my name to the darkening clouds.

The Whole Picture

Smiling
my aunt holds me
in camera range

the pull of my weight
obvious.

Forty years later
my mother
has given me
this piece of myself:

a picture of her absence.

There are no pictures
of them charging her
like a battery

pumping her full
of insulin in 1953.

Someone leaves
a space
someone fills it.

What a photo shows
is what
you do not
see.

Want

1. Doughnuts

She sets aside
the juice glass,
rim gummy
with bits of dough,
scatters holes
on wax paper.
Grease crackles.
Scent of sugar
and cinnamon.
The first melting
bite.
Cold milk.

2. Apple

She holds it
out:
red promise,
slices
it in two,
divides
each half

Marc Frazier

again—
four cradles
on smooth enamel—
scrapes seeds
into the scoured
sink, presses
them into
our similar palms.

What's Missing

Whenever my mom turned on a light switch she said, "Let's put a little light on the subject." She always woke my little sister with, "Morning Glory!" When we were too demanding as children, she asked, "What do you think this is, the Taj Mahal?" On seeing a poor woman she would say, "Poor thing doesn't have a sou to her name." She sat and watched birds flutter around her feeder and read devotions when she grew old. She said less. I have had two hearts in my life: my mother and my little sister. They are both cold now, drifting under the earth like snow.

Thanksgiving with the Homeless Men of Starbucks

> There are ways
> to be lost worse than this one.
> —Carl Phillips

They show some kind of panty hose to one another.
Tricks of the trade to stay warm.
How emasculating, my small self thinks.

Of course my judgment is harsh.
My father worked two, sometimes three,
jobs to support a growing family: 2, 3, 4, 5 kids.
Does the world change this much? This soon?

———

After her death the family fractured like a bad tooth.
Where do we gather now?
What's on my mind is not this poem.

———

In my dream I write:

WILLINGLY

There once was a beautiful lady.
Endless stories begin
like this and lose their way.

Endless shutters close on the past.
In my dream time stops
in all the right places, all the right
faces last.

The Universe Expands

mindless of the balanced and
unbalanced forces of my life

I don't count for much
on the record of matter/space/time

my secrets and regrets
lost in quarks

and particles, my "big bang"
a whimper at the end

My DNA unravels stretches
beyond the moon

while those I love
feel the force of what matters

These Three Remain

—And now abide faith, hope, love, these three; but the
greatest of these is love. 1 Corinthians 13:13

        finger-

tips on backbone   morning waves

in rising light   the sea

the sea   all surface and

memory   metaphor unceasing

how it makes me   want   to confess

how the bones I found   bloomed   in sand

as turtles' eggs   cradled

         below

Marc Frazier

from stasis   wind echoes   the world unabating

pulses   the heart's   energy   in waves

rhythms   a clearing ahead   a caesura

      I   am   poised   for prayer

the silver   evening

ravens drowse   moonlight ripples

ashes rise and de-

scend   roots   reach

a honeycomb hangs   heavy

with what   unholy lips desire

    I feel an old barn col-   lapse

the grace   of many   hands restores it

      as a   blooming   witness

Dog Days

Through the neighbor's yard to the dairy.
Its smell louder than the machinery's clang.
A few coins moist in my closed palm.

The tall red honeysuckles heavy with August drowse,
shallow puddles of afternoon rain.
Heavy air walked through to nightfall.

Breezes through screened windows.
Complaints on the wind.

    Hear ants open peonies, squash blossoms stretch,
    the mare rub her side on the wire fence, the
    hummingbird's wings,
    drone of cicadas.

        Stream of seasons. Wide green lawns of memory.
        Hushed words full. The certain dark.

Danger

> O my catacomb, drifting, my
> drowse-in-honey-until-there's-nothing, nothing
> why be afraid, what are you
> so afraid of?
> —Carl Phillips

From a skyscraper we see the blue water of swimming pools
on top of lower buildings—figures like those in doll houses
    propped up in tiny chairs or lying about on towels.

We sense how this building must give a little, must sway.
When you sing an Irish song about
God holding me in the hollow
    of His hand, I can feel myself giving way like the side

of an ancient ship that can no longer put out from port.
It is no wonder accidents happen.
    It is a wonder any of us live.

II.

Last night in a restaurant, you set your apple next to mine:
two glossy, red skins barely touching. I
remember your nervousness,
    left arm grasping right as if you were checking for a sprain

WILLINGLY

or a break, or testing to see that the bone still lay silent there.
Today sails create resistance to steady wind.
      Fish do not pierce the water's skin in a show of force—

like us, they stay low, prefer the quiet life.
An old Asian woman chases a baby in a bleached diaper;
      quiet lovers fondle inside a giant inner tube.

Teenagers trek to *El Mercado*, flirt in the
road—hands and eyes dart—
little birds picking up scraps along shore.
      The froth amid stones at this end of
      the waves is light as meringue.

I wonder if you know that love is driftwood, untouched,
that I am a loose, white bone floating sharp as stone,
      that you beat n a separate heart.

III.

I hear you in the kitchen whistling for the dog,
looking into the night, the silent concrete.
      I do not know what drives one

to such extremes. I can be many things, including gentle.
But every moment is dangerous. Anything
that happens to one person
      can happen to another.

I will not speak of these things or of the things you are.
For what it is worth, you will never be a face in a crowd,
      a mistake not worth making, a theory proven wrong.

IV.

A beginning is nothing like an end.
We all get places without knowing how.
      Thinking of one thing makes you think of another.

I cannot keep my resolve.
You are many things to me: ice melting,
      change in a blind man's

cup, the slap of a wave on my cheek,
light escaping under the door,
      a far-away, sun-burnt face on white linen.

Little Mexico

Dark figures disappear
      into *El Barrio*'s erotic red,
         into paintings of *conquistadores*.

I listen to the sound of language,
      comforted by my lack of understanding.

If they speak of love here,
      I won't know it.

August

My friend and I lie bathed in bright light.
Children splash, water laps our toes.

I write: *They have linked hair chemistry to acts of violence
but have no idea how two people love or fail to.*

We have only today.
The lives we live could be anyone's.

The drone of motors grows and fades,
repeats itself—an echo we forget to hear.

I'm in love, I say.
We see ducks light as air married to the waves.

Without You

I bring bodies alive with a quarter,
    Watch them laboring
Like pistons and cylinders,
    Without sound.

To unlearn the beauty of you,
    This pornography does best,
Anonymous,
    Ending like all of us—

    A quick click in the dark.

Plea

Morning means anything but promise
Though full of full cups of fresh
My hope as devout as the Pope
Averting his eyes from Vatican violence
O Faith! O Betrayal!
Something new this way comes
Will there be a reward at the end?
Or this, this, this…
Wet water dry drought
A spectrum of good and evil blurs
As the sun tires of the same allusions
Something new this way comes
Days nothing but anticipation
Take my vague feeling of dread
Make of me a sureness something dead

Math

Nearly ninety years fit in this room.
You hold court from a lift chair surrounded
by tokens from the past.

Motherless since birth, you gathered
your grief and moved on.
I water your three plants, exclaim over the
blooming cactus, your green thumb.

I run for sugar-free applesauce, Ensure, Depends.
Fully stocked and little appetite.

Shuffles to the bathroom with a walker.
Pain patches changed religiously.

A wheelchair ride for mashed potatoes and pale meat.
Bed after dinner, rosary in hand.

Like when I was a child I help you with your checkbook:
add up your SS and library pension,

Marc Frazier

subtract your monthly rent for Good Neighbor Care.
How you feared my father catching a mistake.

Remember going for rides, stopping to make
a "visit" at some Catholic church.
You and my sisters covered your unholy heads.

We knelt and prayed separately together.
All this piousness and I just wanted a hand to hold.

What is Left

Below the Green Mountains, I am more stone
than water, my heart a clearing sky.
Cells replicate, grow missing parts.
Writing props: pen point, journal size, pithy
phrases for the dark night of the soul.
Attempts to revive words I've cut fail.
There is no trail back.
Autumn evening.
Flagstones on the road to a house of meaning.
Each Victorian home tucked in by its sashes.
Cicadas dim to backstage hum.
Remember the cottages of Sea Cliff, wild with wisteria and
    blue trim, people gathered to
    watch sun set over the Sound?
My words choke on weeds of want; they grow along every
    unnamed road I find—near
    Caribbean blue, into Santa Fe orange, Vermont green.
Pretty lies bloom, even in desert.
It is always light somewhere to study the errant heart.

The Loss

A blanket poured
over chairs—
a cave;
spread on the ground—
a raft.
A dark crawlspace
stashed a criminal,
someone's name
on his tight lips.

At some point
life lured a blue-eyed
blonde,
hot saxophone, sunny
Saturday, a margarita
in heat.

In other words,
things became
literal,
narrowed into
themselves.
I danced.
The house
stood still.

Into Dark: Cinquains

Given
the world's danger,
beauty. To chart a course
beyond, until the body fails.
Until.
                      Yellow
                      crocus under
                      snow surprises in March.
                      Last leaves lose color, light. Wet wind.
                      Days dim.

To love,
begin again.
Dye flowers for lover,
companion, or the night's desire
to fall.
                      Later,
                      scalpel to lines
                      poet shaped from chaos.
                      Mystery, form, time, the story
                      of us.

Double
helix of life,
bridge of fear into dark.
Stones in water, sliver of moon.
O Death.

Neighbor

Four a.m. wails drag me with her into a hole in the night.
Things crash: clay flower pots shattering?

The sounds of her smashing whatever comes to hand.
Chairs against walls?

The shriek of which animal destroying its den?
This morning she washes windows as if
things only happen in daylight.

I think of rooms constructed with levels
and angles, architect's plans,
of how she kicked the screens out of three TV's.

I want to know how the mind deconstructs,
how buildings outlive us,
if any part of her emerges as something new.

Links

Before the cicadas' August complaints
the long light of the solstice

After ink dries on porous paper
the branching veins of your sketches

Before it furnishes it with grief
good intentions make us a home

After Vermont turns us green
we lose the forest path

Before shopping Buck's County in dusk
coffee under a blue umbrella

After words begin to matter
the silence of: how close can we get?

Before the squawk of an insistent jay
the stillness of tall pines

Marc Frazier

After the coffin is lowered
eyes of the living stare

After what I've come to terms with returns
I sit before the altar I've built

Before days grow longer
early dusk the veil on a mourner's hat

What is Unseen

Not so much the worm, the hook
              Sun bouncing off Lake Ripley
But the little fish reeled in
              Flopping in the boat
Gills miraculous to watch
              The entire idea of life
Retrieving the hook
              Without looking into eyes
My aunt proud of my conquest
              A tiny nearly-dead thing—
That's what childhood is filled with—
              That we slice open
Scraping away guts, rinse
              Grill outside our cabin
While she and her "friend" Pat
              Drink Southern Comfort
As we play badminton and argue
              Like winning matters when we already
Sense that it doesn't
              And practice our swings for thwacking
Lightning bugs in dusk
              Then plop our quarters
For ice cream on the counter
              In the beachside store
Where barely dressed adults

Marc Frazier

                Full of Milwaukee beer
Throw lopsided smiles at us
                From the dark, smelly bar
Confident that each of our fears
                Is real and can undo us
And everyone around us
                Though no one thinks children
Know this, we do, I do
                As I memorize Latin responses
Et cum spiritu tuo,
                As I inhale the scent of wine
harbinger of personal grief to come
                Habemus ad Dominum
As father wipes his fingers
                Daintily on white linen, builds
The house of God by placing
                The square Pall over the chalice
and as I genuflect
                Dignum et justum est
I hear the sunfish gasp

Iterations

There is no limit to the times
a poet can mention the body.
Life is recursive but speaking of it more so:

> *this body that stirs, or fails to*
> *this barely defined shoulder*
> *my body beside someone's but not yet yours*

The perseveration of the artist—
details of a nude, portrait studies.
Language found in the body: *breath, rib, bone.*

> the natural world in the body:
> *your body isn't the restive field it was*
> *the weedy acres of your brow*

Body, exhausted by metaphor—limited, earthbound.
Words can't capture how it falters, breaks,
how there may be something more.

> and if spirit exists—
> do I open the window and let it fly?
> create words for the body's fresh landscape of death?

Christmas Eve

pines heave in white

line the broad avenues of regret
               longing

the words of poets, myth:
                      deeper wells

crisp smell of winter
       breath hot inside a scarf

(what we were told taken back
      again and again)

what did I mean to say

before the white hills of December
before the long road back from yesterday

Again

Every morning
you forget you live.
Every morning
starts the same
though you're not
the same.

Some mornings a dream
sticks in your web.
You lure it out.
Inspect it. Sometimes
it vanishes, sometimes
not.

Every morning
you have things to do.
Some mornings
you imagine
having nothing
to do.

Try doing nothing
for a day.
The depressed know how.
Try holding your breath
and live.

The Waves

The sun a large yellow globe focused on us like the delight of youth. In the dust on the windy hill it appeared like a real hope. Mostly this world, I thought, looking down at ants and other insects scrambling for their sustenance, is a terrible affair. My pear-shaped eyes squinted as the sun rose and my friend Molly sighed. "Look at the islands of cloud," she exclaimed, but I was already moving on. "Let us explore," I said, lifting my skirt to reveal boots made for walking. We knew we were close to the sea for we could smell it in the air. Coming over a steep hill I looked down at its large landscape of buried life. We began our trek down to the shore, hurrying like children. Daringly, we took off our boots and stockings and felt the cool splash wash over us. What measureless abundance lurks below I reflected as a thought for my writing came to me. More time should be spent exploring its depths than sending explorers to the Arctic to founder in the ice. The seabirds scavenged along shoreline, picking especially at anything freshly dead. These birds, like poets—scapegoats bloody in tooth and claw. How is it that life is good as often as it is? We wandered along the beach until shadows lengthened and we began to wander back to where the path back up the hill lay. I started to hurry for a chill and a creeping sensation akin to horror overtook me at the thought of facing the winds of darkness. What a confusion! All of this. Is there a father to the sea? But I knew all was

WILLINGLY

natural gestation. The wave rises within us, undistinguishable from want, and we rise to the occasion.

—from a small group of
three-word phrases in the novel

Stories, Café Voltaire

The solstice is almost here.
I wrote a poem by that title.
It was about loss, which surprised no one.
I almost mailed you a book. About loss.
But also salvation. The woman goes home with her baby.
On a train. To her father. Everyone is damaged but alive.

Except her husband who dies in an auto wreck.

If I mail you the book, I will not show
you this poem until later.
I am surprised I told you the ending.
I wanted to hear it for some reason,
though I am discomfited by it.
These days my mind works farther and farther ahead of itself:
a plot line gone haywire.
The author's voice is the ocean echoing along shore

bearing some inevitability I cannot accept.

Another ending disturbs me: a woman,
American, dazed from experience,
heat, leaves her cab and wanders into the
maze of a North African town.
The people who've come to retrieve her discover she is gone.

WILLINGLY

She does not want to be saved.
Which is more disquieting: that this is no ending,

or that I understand why she does it?

The woman next to me is bald. By choice.
I think of chemo patients who dream hair.
Across from her is a man who writes frantically in a book,
scribbles between line after line of copyrighted print.
I think of the author, how critical each word was,

how one way, or another, we make stories fit.

Willingly

The swish of corn stalks lulls as night
crawlers slither in a wet dawn.
We pilfer sugar cubes for the mare sniffing over the fence,

still, drawn in by her heavy, chestnut eyes—her elegance.
We capture what earth yields: beetles,
ants, garter snakes, our futures,

dig to China with a kitchen spoon
terrified that foreign eyes gaze up.
Asleep on the porch floor when heat takes
over, every noise is a danger.

We scare one another through the
night until mother fixes eggs,
hurries us to the dairy, bringing back its milky odor with us.

Each whines for the farm on Sunday—to run
forever and ride on Harry's tractor.
Autumn's smell of burning leaves on our skin,
we rake leaf patterns on the ground:

a child's blueprint of a house: each raked-out space a room.
On my back in a "bedroom," I study a giant
branch, its fingers reaching into winter.

WILLINGLY

As day ends I enter a warmer house
where I gaze out my window
at the moon, convinced I've chosen this life.

Taken

Tornado

Banded newspapers thud on porches
as sky darkens to a green dream.
By candlelight, voices on the radio:
*Has anyone seen a boy, fair-haired, 11,
birthmark on his chin; a woman, 30, red-haired, tall?*
Our parents look at us as if we've just arrived,
or are leaving.

For Sale

Already it is not ours.
We abandon it for hours, return like thieves.
Was this door shut? Did they touch this?
Strangers paced steps we left behind.
Someone climbed stairs to my room,
a spy committing it to memory.

Kidnapped

Bobby speaks her exotic name: *Maria*,
syllables escaping like a tease.
He tells her story, or is it?

WILLINGLY

I see a car slowing, hear the house-by-house search.
Detail by detail, she comes alive:
Walnut Street, in the snow, after school.
I hear her play in the attic.
I turn a corner, she smiles at me.

The Trip to Uncle Harry's Funeral

> But we remain, touching a wound
> That opens to our richest horror.
> —"Auto Wreck," Karl Shapiro

the family in two cars
my sister and I in the back of one
our silent grandfather rides shotgun
his aftershave smells of old age
it should be him in a coffin
our brother in his dark suit drives us deeper into the country
should we listen to music?
      is that our parents' car off to the side of the road?
      My brother veers onto the shoulder
      our sister Mary hunches over a man thrown
      from a turned-over, rickety truck
      she tries in vain to keep him alive
      with her new nursing skills
      our small selves cannot imagine this
      under the truck lies a woman on her back
      with the truck's weight upon her
      she looks cut in two like a magician's assistant
      you can tell she is dead from behind car windows
our grief grows small or large

WILLINGLY

soon we will kneel before the casket where
Harry is finished with farm chores
smelling of death Mary will hug Aunt Rita
whose long hair swirls atop her head like something final

Theorem

> If you suffer, it's not because things are impermanent.
> It's because you believe things are permanent.
> —Thich Nat Hahn

How many prayers stop in the throat?
How many doves coo in the church square?

A novel begins: *I don't know how I should live.*
I don't know how anyone should live.

Is this true?
Elmore Leonard said, *If it sounds like writing, I rewrite it.*

It is hard to believe in anyone.
It is hard to believe in.

It is hard to believe.
It is hard.

Life reduces like an algebraic equation.
Picasso could make anything into art.

Did all of it matter?
Do my words?

WILLINGLY

How much time is left in which to matter?
Summer is ending.

When does fall begin?
What makes one day worth more?

That certain slant of light?
It makes sense to like paintings of cloudy
skies better than those of clear ones.

Virginia Woolf tries to capture one moment.
Then another.

Buddha said to consider his teaching to be
a raft helping you to the other shore.
When my mother was dying she looked me
in the eyes and asked, *Am I dying?*

Listen

Let the wolf metaphor stand. Must I heed what some editor says about cliché. They see them everywhere: tone deaf to the sounds of poems: their boxcar rhythm. Occasionally, they astound with a miraculously astute observation. For decades, I let them throw me into bouts of depression, for they were the only route. Was I cursed to be able to hear the world? Once for a week I was obsessed with the words of osteology: epiphysis, apophysis. I take words upstairs to empty halls where I let them echo. When Michael took sick, there was a polite buffer of silence between the world and me. I cared for him and felt guilty pursuing my passion for language play. When the morphine did little I knew what was coming. Each night I whispered to myself, God don't let that happen tonight. I would read aloud to him at all hours of the night. Sometimes I would put my face up close to him and think, *it's still him*. I couldn't help but reminisce to myself about the stories he told of growing up, of his family living in an unfinished basement. My mind wandered madly. I doodled on my unlined journal's pages: a cross within a circle with distinct dots around the circumference. It reminded me of Southwest petrographs, of our time exploring the spiritual sites of northern New Mexico. After he passed, I convinced myself there was nothing in creation that is a home. I took up sadness. It took a couple of years for language to speak to me again. One day huddled in a winter coat and scarf jotting down thoughts on a park bench I thought: at one time

WILLINGLY

in this world it was alright to throw a kiss to a pretty stranger. This world speaks more than ever, and there has never been a time when there is so little rich language to hear.

—written from phrases and lines from the same page number of fourteen different books

Prayer in Winter

> The sun rises under the pillar of your tongue.
> —Sylvia Plath

How many times can they put you together:
All the king's horses and all the king's men
labor over you with their pumps,

and tubes, and catheters and their glue
as we wait in a barren field, cold and uninformed
and guessing what can happen to the body

broken and broken again, the brain refusing not to seize
like a Mexican jumping bean?
We wait, transcribe their messages as best we can

like we could, finally, understand,
but there is too much wildness in the world for that.
This January nothing thaws,

the roots our buried thoughts.
Sparrows rethink their choices: here, there.

infinitives

to sleep in the womb of a shell
    in a forest of symbols
      with ancient wounds

caress an infant's little finger
    the weak kitten
      the hands of a sculptor

enter the forbidden passage
    a new personality
      the black boat

reenter the secrets of young summers
    the odors of infancy
      the sadness of beauty

see gravity
    a hidden city
      the breath of a ghost

Marc Frazier

remember every window
     the first words of mother
     the warm belly of desire

cross the frontier into madness
     the sea to a new world
     the night to a fatal dawn

gather broken moons
     the disappearing surf
     the silent cries of miscarriages

to love
     to love
     to love

Song of Songs

Your eyes are doves in my heart.
Your still lips a work of art.

Leagues beneath the sea they chart
the Earth's trembling so that ships may steer.

Cloudy midnights don't obscure my heart.
What is the source then of this fear?

Nothing can transform us like time apart.
Or seeing the future look back with a sneer.

Diana's bare feet stalked the wary hart.
When all good and bad lay in the celestial sphere.

I mean these words solely to impart
the hope you shall ever be near.

Place me like a seal over your heart.
Show me, my beauty, where to start.

Remainders

Aunt Bertha's thick ankles tucked in orthopedic shoes,
she stirs water into flour for chicken gravy paste.

The soon-to-be-closed eyes of my father
stare at the dog planter on the window ledge.

Mother's hands run fabric under the jumpy needle,
the machine's drone luring me to love.

The voice of great-uncle John's deep bass
volleys with Esther's small, squeaky refrains.

Nicks on Sergio's perfect face
held like a calla between my flowering palms.

The smell of Sunday's roast with onions
potatoes and carrots waft through register vents.

Grandfather's sad, wrinkled red face
dozes alone in the paneled TV room.

David of the Espanola Valley places his hand over mine
as I look above the table at New Mexican stars.

I cannot recall her last smile here beside the unplugged
body as the doctor says. "She's passed."

Painting of Woman, Café Express

Huge legs dangle over my table.

She reminds me of living close to ground:

painting on the floor, napping on a rug—

primary people above me like this blue

and green lady.

Life fades.

Color is.

Settling

Like anyone I need to be inspired. I walk along the lake by all the dead-end streets where the Mexicans live. As the day wears on, a few of them ramble down by the water to *la bodega, la cantina* to buy beer and Doritos, cigarettes. It is one of those times without women. The point of anything is never the apparent fact. The cars are not the point at all.

When I moved here, I stood on the phone by the White Hen for hours at a time, the locals wondering if I was mad, the long-haired girl behind the counter puzzled by my longevity. She made change, that's all. It was Saturday or Sunday.

I watched the cord as if it were alive, could get even, switched the phone from one ear to the other. It was like trying on clothes, shopping for shoes. Words coiled. None of them fit. *The connection is bad*, I lied. Making excuses for my tendency to wander, to see other sides.

This personal drama reduced itself like an algebraic equation into a more reasoned perspective. That is how life is spent: reducing lies to logic. I go on. Because I have learned to. Because life, like anything is a habit, can be found almost anywhere, can happen to anyone.

Over a Dark Lake

—alternating lines from *The Man with Night Sweats*
and *Little Gidding* without edits or additions

I.

I was delivered into time again come
forth into sun as if without a past

in the dark time of the year
I think of Oedipus, old, led by a boy in windless cold

the brief sun flames the ice on pond and ditches
my flesh was its own shield:

where it was   gashed   it healed
now the hedgerow is blanched for an hour

with transitory blossom of snow
the smooth red body of a young madrone
the brown hillside where light grows   and fades
the sound of the voice praying   now you are a bag of ash
scattered on a coastal ridge   all the ash burnt roses leave

II.

of course the dead outnumber us—how their
recruiting armies grow! there is no earth smell
or smell of living thing how can I continue
I asked? when I left my body on a distant shore
the year of grief being through (a shell, a husk
of meaning) the peace of trees that all night whisper
nothings but heard half heard in the stillness
between two waves of the sea

could that be what it meant?
this is the death of water and fire

III.

as if hands were enough to hold an avalanche off it
would be the same at the end of the journey

if you came at night like a broken king dark as a
gypsy, berry-brown with dirt tender loin and

glands   delicate almost as eyeballs a bloom more
sudden than that of summer neither budding

nor fading his genitals as neat as a stone acorn
with its two oak leaves and what the dead had

no speech for when living or side by side and
touching at the hips as if we were two trees bough

grazing bough tongued with fire beyond the language
of the living   repeated all day through

in the sexual longings of the spring all shall be
well and all manner of thing shall be well

Crossings

> No matter whose bed you die in
> the bed will be yours
> for your voyage…
> —Anne Sexton

We maneuver city crosswalks and don't collide
radar guides us as we

enter into no man's land and back during warfare
or over to some banal hatred.

I know the border of madness,
drugged back as

a fish deboned by night,
a purple hedge going to seed.

Boards from my childhood creak.
Dawn, I turn on. A light. Also a leaf, I turn toward it.

All but one image of beauty slid from Aschenbach,
and two breathtaking syllables: Ta-dzio.

Marc Frazier

In the end, the sea will take me like a rose,
that, now, can be handled.

I ride this last bed, rising to the mouth of God's moon.
There will be no questions, no password given.

In Judgment's place: bang bang, knock knock,
the madman's thrum.

Once upon a Time

We ate rabbit for dinner.
This story saddened me most of all.
Cynthia the psychic asks: *How have you*
gotten this far with one oar?
Old Miss Tilford pulled books out of a battered,
upholstery bag like a good witch.
Any story would do.
In school I believed a thin, gruel-like self
propped up by the alphabet.
I stopped responding to my name.
They thought I could not hear them but I could.
You are one of the watched ones, she adds.
I became my mother's story, unable to respond to
myself as she could not respond to me. Valium's
lovely blue notes became my lullaby.
Cynthia in her ballet slippers dances in
the airy loft between readings.
Halifax is full of parables of drowning.
When there I spoke in a language heard only by the dead,
     found words in an old can by a chips wagon and began
         again, my past as loud as silence in a Bergman movie.
The tale of recovery does not end.
My life remains narrowed by what I can't accept.

Marc Frazier

So much depends on who does the telling.
I dream spring, a long life, fear I will be loved.
Who is
watching who
deserves to be

The Rock

I cross stones, shells to touch the face of God:
This colossus pierces *Golf de St. Laurent*—a magnet,

a friable giant withstanding centuries.
No matter where I stand below, I see only part.

The view from Lookout Point gives context, a spiritual
light: a huge white cross secured by
cables, wildflowers, grasses.

Here you crossed to a wider blue, guided by gulls.
Bold colors rustle in wind—your
flowers; this cross—your faith.

I must let you go. We never understood one another's God.
I remember counting money hour
after hour (*in lieu of flowers*),

the trail of food from people I did not
know, sitting through communion,
eyes burning the back of my head.
I believe in the power of goodbye.

Progression

                    cento from my book *Each Thing Touches*

the seawall groans
a sound like willows in distress

memory stuck in the ruin of my move
seaward
silt at the edge of shore

        if we were listened to it was chance
        the map of childhood safe in our heads:

        among swirls of snow, winter light
        we studied only what was before us
        limbs not knowing the body's nature

when man saw sky, he knew he was mortal
there are no gods without death
the shape of what once lived

        I do not have one life

ants open peonies as if souls will emerge

WILLINGLY

Coleus throbs:
my words lean like leaves toward light

        a new race would do everything the same
        any ending does fine

Acknowledgments

"Iterations," italicized lines by Carl Phillips and Sylvia Plath

List of Credits

The following poems previously appeared in the following publications:

"November Evenings, Southern Illinois," *Rhino*; "Sergio," *The Outrider Review*; "Taken," *English Journal*; "awakening," "expose," "Once upon a Time," *f(r)iction*; "I Am Aware,"*OCHO*; "Appositives," *Kentucky Review*; "The Whole Picture," *Iodine Poetry Journal*; "Without Words," "What is Unseen," *Wilderness House Literary Review*; "Little Mexico," "Without You," *The Miscreant*; "Thanksgiving with the Homeless Men of Starbucks," *The Good Men Project*; "Danger," *The Literati Quarterly*; "Over a Dark Lake," "architecture," *BlazeVOX16*; "infinitives," *Crack the Spine*; "Theorem," *Blue Fifth Review*; "Prayer in Winter," *South Florida Poetry Journal*; "little death: dissociative identity," *The Gay and Lesbian Review*; "Geography Lessons," "What is Left," *The Blue Nib*; "Christmas Eve," "Then," *Off the Rocks*; "Math," *Indigent Press*; "If It Comes to That," *Bird's Thumb*; "The Loss, "*River Oak Review*; "Settling," *PinchPenny*; "The Rock," *Aeolian Harp Anthology, Volume 3*; "Iterations," "synopsis," *Visual Artists Collective*; "Stories, Café Voltaire," *Pirene's Fountain*; "Meditation One," *MayDay Magazine*; "Willingly," *Bluestem* "Crossings," *Picaroon Poetry*; "The Trip to Uncle Harry's Funeral," *The Pangolin Review*"; "Heart Tide," "A Brief Journey: Double Etheree," "Into Dark: Cinquains," *Gold Wake Live*; "Dakota, Illinois," *After Happy Hour Review*; "Abide with Me," *Adirondack Review*; "Links," "Progression," *Sheila-Na-Gig*; "Listen," *Burningword Literary Journal*; "Do Not Weep," *Poetry Quarterly*; "Again," *The Drabble*.

About the Author

Marc Frazier has published poetry in journals including *The Spoon River Poetry Review, ACM, Good Men Project, f(r)iction, The Gay and Lesbian Review, Slant, Permafrost, Plainsongs, English Journal, Ascent, BlazeVox,* and *Poet Lore* among many others. Memoir excerpts from his book *WITHOUT* have been published in *Gravel, The Good Men Project, decomP, Autre, Cobalt Magazine, Evening Street Review,* and *Punctuate*. A poetry folio was accepted for the *Aeolian Harp Series: anthology of poetry folios* Volume Three 2017 (Glass Lyre Press). The poem "What Lies Hidden" was chosen for inclusion in *New Poetry from the Midwest* (New American Press). Marc, the recipient of an Illinois Arts Council Award for poetry, has been featured on *Verse Daily* and has been nominated for a Pushcart Prize and a "best of the net." His first book *The Way Here* and two chapbooks are available on Amazon as well as a second full-length collection titled *Each Thing Touches* (Glass Lyre Press). The leader of numerous writing workshops in the Chicago area and participant in numerous poetry readings, Marc has had writing residencies at Vermont Studio Center and the Ragdale Foundation in addition to publishing poetry book reviews and editing literary publications. A retired teacher who also taught in the education department of a major Chicago university, he has been involved with school improvement efforts as a certified school improvement specialist. Marc, originally from rural northwestern Illinois, resides in Oak Park, Illinois but enjoys spending as much time as possible in the winter near the ocean in South Florida. He serves on the board of NewTown Writers, possibly the longest continual LGBTQ+ writing workshop and publishing venue in the nation which began in the early 1980's. Marc is active on social media, particularly Facebook. His website is www.marcfrazier.org.

www.ingramcontent.com/pod-product-compliance
Lightning Source LLC
Chambersburg PA
CBHW030123100526
44591CB00009B/502